T0194630

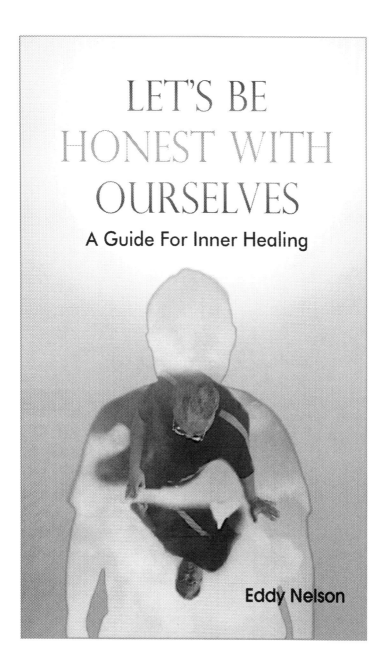

LET'S BE HONEST WITH OURSELVES

A Guide For Inner Healing

Eddy Nelson

WESTBOW
PRESS®
A DIVISION OF THOMAS NELSON
& ZONDERVAN

Second Edition

Author's direct contact: hon457236@gmail.com

WestBow Press books may be ordered through booksellers or by contacting:

WestBow Press
A Division of Thomas Nelson & Zondervan
1663 Liberty Drive
Bloomington, IN 47403
www.westbowpress.com
1 (866) 928-1240

WestBow Press rev. date: 5/20/2019

Book Cover: Mario Chambers
Graphic Designer Xpress Color — Mario@xpresscolor.com

Barracks Editorial and Design House, LLC.
iambevtheeditor@gmail.com

ISBN: 978-1-9736-6179-5 (sc)
ISBN: 978-1-9736-6163-4 (e)

DEDICATION

This is dedicated to my Great Grandma, Lucinda Cabral, who made such a Godly impact on me throughout my life.

To my wife, Kareen Coke Nelson, for her much needed collaboration in putting this book together.

In appreciation of Apostle Yvette Brinson, the co-pastor of my home church, Redeeming Word Christian Center International, who through one sermon, helped me to realize I needed to be honest with myself.

TABLE OF CONTENTS

INTRODUCTION

L et's Be Honest With Ourselves. Have you ever struggled with identifying who you are or knowing your self-worth? This book will help you to discover your purpose, find your truth, accept it, and reconnect you with God's original plan for your life and propel you further into your destiny.

There are people everywhere all over the world in villages, towns, and cities who can identify with this on some level. They are actively engaged with this relentless undertaking of truth. I will also discuss my personal experiences in hopes that my transparency will align you closer to your truth.

Let's start with a simple definition to awaken your reality: *honest*— "*being free of deceit and untruthfulness.*" And the adjective is: to be sincere, candid, frank, direct and open about the truth. What truth? The truth about your feelings and emotions and understanding of who you are inside. Who you pretend to be or the hidden you that no one sees or knows. Have you wept about what you find ugly about yourself? The ugly things about you that you focus on without seeing the true beauty and value God has placed within you? Are you bothered by seeing the wonderful lives people around you are living? Or the beautiful pictures of places you desire to go and the family you long for; the real you is authentic, and no one else can copy your personality, smile, or purpose.

You're an Original Masterpiece created before you were even formed in the womb, *bona fide* and born to live—sealed with God's stamp of approval on this earth! I need you to pay attention so that you may bring forward the truth from inside of you. Seize this moment to search inside and highlight what makes you who you are.

We go through life believing that honesty is not the best policy because the truth is not always accepted. Absolutely! One thing that I do know; the real you want to unfold like a beautiful butterfly. There is a saying and it is truth to those who choose not to understand or obey. The saying is, *"You can't handle the truth."* Maybe you can't handle what you don't understand. Once you fully understand then YES, you can! Oh, you're probably saying, *"You have not seen my past, you are not walking in my shoes and you don't know my life!"*

Wait for it… Let me explain, everything you have gone through has *not* been pointless. You can learn and move on because your best life is in front of you. Yes—I said you! Keep it moving and keep living it forward. I see a smile, maybe a little disbelief, but I do sense hope springing forward.

Is it easy to follow the crowd and do what is accepted and not be true to yourself? Why be different and do what is right when I can fit in and not be noticed within the crowd? You know the crowd is not always right, but you as an individual, must stand alone for what is right.

People with high self-esteem believe they are worthy of love and don't question how someone feels about them. They know that they are good, competent, and lovable and trust that the right person for them will see them as valuable.

Confident people know what they will, and will not accept; and don't allow themselves to be pressured into doing things they don't want to do. Now, if this does not sound like you, well it will be; if you desire to do the hard work. It may not happen overnight, but with daily practice you will find yourself.

Your responsibility is to find your purpose and live it out loud so that you fulfill your destiny for yourself and for those you are called to impact. It is the Creator's desire for you and your family to prosper, but also to give back to anyone in need. Your life is to mirror the expressed Image of His Love through our Savior.

No one lives just for himself; your legacy will continue long after your death. People will always remember how you made them feel; and how well you conducted your life will forever be in the hearts of all who knew or heard about you after you're gone. Let's be frank and straightforward about how your life matters;

get yourself together, and identify what He ordained for you to accomplish in life.

You are unique and so loved by Him—we are all waiting for you to see your worth! Your truth is worth fighting for, so we need to get to the root of your struggle; let's start by opening up where you are in your life.

CHAPTER 1
Identifying Where You Are

Think on this. What are you saying today about your narrative (your past, your life story) and how are you ultimately presenting yourself to others?

Your thoughts are a product or the result of who you are or will become. Are you present physically, but mentally living in the past? Are you angry, sad, or happy inside? Are you revealing to us what you are inside? What were you created to fulfill on earth? Are you willing to trust the Creator to bring forth the TRUE you He formed?

The first thing that stops people from living a life that's authentic is the fact that they never define or become clear on what's true to them. They never become clear on what their own deepest values are and what's meaningful to them.

Your values dictate how you live your life and the things that are important to you. When what you do and the way you behave match your values, life is usually good and you're satisfied. However, when these don't align with your personal values, that's when things feel wrong.

Do you set standards for your relationships with people or do you accept what others do or say? Do you have a personal evolving relationship with God?

The second thing that stops people from living their truth is a lack of awareness or mindfulness. Living fully in the present moment means that your awareness is completely centered on the here and now. You are not worrying about the future or thinking about the past. When you live in the present, you are living where life is happening.

Without mindfulness, we often fall into mechanical patterns of thought and behavior, most of which we did not consciously choose and most of which were handed down to us from our culture and upbringing. Living in unawareness like this leads to a sense of discontent and disconnection from ourselves.

If you are finding yourself, you must accept yourself above all else. Loving yourself is finding peace within yourself and resting comfortably as a result of discovering that peace. It is very human to feel sad, hurt, and afraid sometimes. It's a sign of strength, not weakness, to become mindful of these feelings and allow a friendly space for them.

Resolve to make peace with who you are so you can show the world the best part of you. Connect to your heart (core) which is the innermost or most intimate part of you. Finding purpose of life is to find the reason you were created to live and then live it. Purpose will guide life decisions, influence behavior, shape goals, offer a sense of direction and create meaning. You can't think your way into finding your life; you have to make your way into it. The more action you take in finding your life the clearer things will become.

Ask yourself—what do you love? Start taking steps to do what you love and follow the leading of your heart because it is the best tool to access your true purpose and passion. Your heart will naturally be more joyful and motivated to explore. Let go of thinking there is only one purpose for you and embrace the idea that our purpose in life is to love life fully!

For example, try new foods or new things; resist the unknown and engage in what is happening right here and now—where you are. Don't go out on the edge with something new without researching and being fully prepared for the outcome. I'm referring to something new like if you enjoy only singing or listening to rap or country music; try listening to jazz.

If you only love watching or playing basketball, try tennis or ice skating. If there is something you really enjoy doing, create a blog or YouTube video and teach it. This may not be your purpose, but your passion will lead you to it. Try to be present at all times and enjoy the journey—remember, daily action equals a purposeful life.

John 8:32— says, *"And ye shall know the truth, and the truth shall make you free."*

Maybe the idea of knowing truth is scary and could leave a bad taste in your mouth. Some people say they don't want to know truth because knowing may hurt. Whatever your reason, why is it that you cannot seem to overcome the unknown by not knowing?

The truth is honesty, and God can only work through truth—not the lies we tell ourselves.

Your Family

Matthew 10:36— says, *"And a man's foes shall be they of his own household."*

Understand, your family has issues that quite possibly run deep in your life. There is truth to the saying, *"You are a product of your environment."* Identifying behavior is essential to breaking any generational traits and ending the cycle with you. You will also need to understand if your identity struggle stems from your upbringing or from yourself.

Let's start with generational traits that are not considered good behavior:

According to *www.wikipedia.org* a **dysfunctional family** *"is a family in which conflict, misbehavior, child neglect or abuse on the part of individual parents occurs continuously and regularly, leading other members to accommodate such actions."* Many people hope that once they leave home, they will leave their family and childhood problems behind.

However, many find that they experience similar problems, as well as, similar feelings and relationship patterns long after they have left the family environment. Ideally, when children grow up in family environments which help them feel worthwhile and valuable, they learn that their feelings and needs are important and can be expressed.

Children growing up in such supportive environments are likely to form healthy, open relationships in adulthood. However, families may fail to provide for many of their children's emotional and physical needs.

In addition, the families' communication patterns may severely limit the child's expressions of feelings and needs.

Children growing up in such families are likely to develop low self-esteem and feel that their needs are not important or perhaps should not be taken seriously by others. As a result, they may form unsatisfying relationships as adults.

My Family

My mother married three times. First to my dad, but he died when I was three years old. Therefore, I do not remember him; I wish I had memories. I do remember, however, having a need to be mentored by a man. Only a man can connect with another man to understand and confirm what it means to be a man. Well, both of mom's other husband's only connection to me was her and not as a male role model.

I experienced growing up without a dad, and as my relationship with God developed, I learned to give Him those feelings of neglect. Through this experience, I recognized the importance of being reared in a healthy family environment and the need of a loving dad.

A dysfunctional family environment whether direct or indirect, will have an undesirable learned behavior. I used to be a heavy drinker for a number of years because that is what my male role models did, however, I saw the effects it produced in them, so I stopped. Acknowledging there is an issue is the first step to recovery.

If you have to talk to a counselor to address your issues, he or she will challenge you to open up and expose the unknown truth. It is a journey you have to walk out daily until you are able to manage the path.

Forgiveness is the process of healing and the path to peace within yourself is the ultimate goal. You can't be forgiven if you don't forgive your family for their dysfunction.

Purpose in your mind to not focus on what a person does, but see the cry for help without being offended. Let it go and be free from the bondage of slavery that un-forgiveness feeds. The root of most fights, crimes, anger or hatred stems from un-forgiveness. Own up to your family's dysfunction and focus on a plan of action for your life.

CHAPTER 2
What You Don't Like About Yourself

Physical Appearance

Psalms 139:14—says, *"I will praise thee; for I am fearfully and wonderfully made:* marvellous *are* thy works; and *that* my soul knoweth right well."

We should all be in awe of our Creator God, as He made each of us in His own Image and gave us dominion and authority. As we develop a relationship with Him and learn to reverence His great Power, then we will discover how wonderfully made we really are as David so eloquently says it in the above Psalms. Our perception of ourselves is expressed in knowing our true identity and as we communicate, our demeanor will become contagious to others.

What is it you don't like about yourself? Have you ever looked at yourself in the mirror and just didn't like what you saw? I don't know about you, but I definitely have. David was royalty before he was given the title of King. You and I are also royalty, but until we are *honest with ourselves* and take our rightful place in Him, we can't stand and reflect our God given truth.

As a young child, it was discovered that I had issues with my hearing and was made to wear hearing aids to improve my hearing. There were times I would not wear them because it wasn't perceived well by my peers not to mention, kids can be very cruel. I felt different and was very uncomfortable, and the perception I had of myself was one of feeling *retarded*. So, I stopped wearing them for a while because I wanted to feel and look normal like everyone and be accepted by my peers and family.

But without my hearing device, it forced me to read lips, which I wasn't very good at. Because of this, it took so much more energy to learn and I struggled with my self-confidence, as I often mis-heard and mis-read people's lips; which only hindered my communication skills and hearing abilities.

Later in life after I was married and with children, I heard that many celebrities achieved success with their hearing disability. This truth allowed me to open up and feel more accepted and comfortable socially with my hearing loss.

Insecurity

The lack of confidence in one's self is a terrible way to live, but God wants you to be confident in your ability in Him.

Approval of Others

When you put your faith in man instead of God, it will lead you to disappointment. Man will fail you, but God won't so, trusting God means safety.

Song of Solomon 4:7— NIV says, *"You are altogether beautiful, my darling; there is no flaw in you."*

Is there a physical aspect such as your face, feet, breast or other bodily features you don't like? Did you inherit a nose or eyes you would like to have surgically enhanced or changed?

There are people who go through life obsessed with their weight, height or beauty. For the most part, you can make the necessary changes and lose weight, enhance your smile, buy new clothes or change your hairstyle, etc. These are all simple and affordable changes that will boost your self-esteem; apart from that, learn to love or embrace the features you can't change.

Sometimes it seems easier to love others than it does to love yourself, but self-acceptance is an important part of developing healthy relationships with others. With a little practice and patience; you can learn to love yourself too. To learn to love yourself, practice reframing events in your life in a positive light, and don't worry about trying to be perfect.

Reframing is a way of viewing and experiencing events, ideas, concepts and emotions to find more positive alternatives. Instead of allowing outside opinions to affect how you see yourself, focus on the things you like about yourself and keep working towards your goals. Make a list of your positive attributes and reflect on them daily.

Many people have trouble letting go of negative thoughts that they have about themselves. These negative thoughts often come from outside people whose opinion we value and from whom we seek love and acceptance.

Self-Pity

God only responds to our faith; wallowing in self-pity is a form of worshipping yourself. This type of behavior prevents the wisdom of God from having an impact because it's continually blocked by the *"poor me"* attitude.

Selfishness

Living a life centered on you and your survival is not God's perfect will for you. Selfishness can be an extremely difficult giant to take down. The Bible says, *"the greatest among us is one who serves or servant-hood."*[1]—***paraphrased***. So, how about putting yourself

---

[1] *But he that is greatest among you shall be your servant.* —Matthew 23:11-KJV

on the shelf and live a life dedicated to loving and serving others?

Lazy Thinking

Your thought life is a powerful tool, so much so that, *"we become what we continually think on."* Don't just find solutions to problems that take the least mental effort; this really isn't thinking or deliberating because real thinking requires attention and effort. Look in the mirror and whatever you don't like about yourself, make confessions and speak the opposite of what you see. Even if you have to speak it over yourself every day until it resonates and take root in your mind and spirit.

Our human bodies are the most complex and unique organism in the world, and that complexity and uniqueness speaks volumes about the mind of its Creator. The incredible nature of our entire physical bodies, every aspect of the body, down to the tiniest microscopic cell, reveals that you are Awesome.

CHAPTER 3
Recognize What Was Said About You

James 3:10—says, *"Out of the same mouth come praise and cursing. My brothers and sisters, this should not be."*

What words have you or others spoken over your life that have governed your destiny for the better or has left a negative affect? I spent years not recognizing how words spoken over my life have influenced me. It wasn't until I became much older that I realized I did not deal with unkind words aptly. Instead, I simply blocked them and pretended that negative words were not my truth.

Most of them were not really my truth, but I had to release those negative words that affected my truth. In other words, I convinced myself that I was ok, but really, I wasn't. Unfortunately, children do not understand how impactful their words can be whether positive or negative which can leave their peers affected for years or a lifetime. It is what you say and how you say it that leaves a lasting impact on others.

I suffered verbal abuse from my peers in elementary through high school. Words like *"you are an ugly dude."* Seasoned with insults like *"your Mom can't afford to buy you stylish clothes."* My Mother did not consult with me about the style of clothes she purchased; I wore whatever she liked and spent her money on. Then there was the issue of my hearing aids; children would stare because I did not look like them. So, I suffered the insults and the stares as a result of my fashionable wardrobe and hearing aids. This aided in lowering my self-esteem, and as a result I did not wear the hearing aids. I was struggling within myself because I did not know who I was.

People who are inclined to put others down, usually have personal issues themselves and suffer with low-self-esteem; so, don't let their words harm you. When people are secure with themselves and know who they are, I can guarantee, self-esteem is not an issue. Instead, they will usually speak words of encouragement that will uplift and motivate you. If you are overcoming negative words spoken over you or self-inflicted words or thoughts, it's time to renew your mind with the Word of God. Remember, you are special; negative words cannot keep you down unless you allow it.

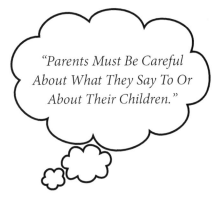

"Parents Must Be Careful About What They Say To Or About Their Children."

Ephesians 4:29— says,

> *"Let no corrupt communication proceed out of your mouth, but that which is good to the use of edifying, that it may minister grace unto the hearers."*

Teach your children the practice of good communication that will edify and build up others. If you don't practice this with your children they may grow up self-centered, dysfunctional and this behavior will be the norm. As a father and man of God, I understood the importance of the spoken word, so I encouraged my children and always spoke well to and about them. My mother, however, had not grasped this truth because she was unapologetic about whatever came out of her mouth.

Later in life, in speaking to other people, I came to realize that my mother's negative words were a result of her cultural upbringing. She was raised in a culture where the norm was for parents to be highly critical and harsh towards their children. If I had known then, what I know now, I would have been better prepared to release her negative words as a child and be free from its results.

My mother would speak over me saying, *"You will never marry because you are hard of hearing and no woman will ever want you." And, should you marry, s*he would say, *"Your wife will cheat because you cannot hear well, and she will take advantage of you."* Things that were spoken out of her own insecurities was her truth, and did not hold true; nevertheless, it left me doubtful for a while.

I forgave her years ago because I recognized that her words were marred by her hurt and lifestyle choices. I encourage you to go beyond your hurt and live in the present so you can clearly see what is best for your child's life, your legacy and the next generation. Remember, as parents, we are our children's first teachers and our words are creating a lasting impact throughout their life. So, don't engage in conversation that's not intended to build confidence because it reflects where you are and your truth.

CHAPTER 4

Fear

2 Timothy 1:7— *"For God hath not given us the spirit of fear; but of power, and of love, and of a sound mind."*

Fear is a strong unpleasant emotion caused by anticipation or awareness of danger. I have struggled with doubt, fear, and wavering confidence.

Regardless of where you are in your life, I pray that the Spirit of God will touch you as it has touched me. Our Heavenly Father truly does love us, and has the ability and the desire to help us overcome doubts and fears in our lives. Fear doesn't come from God, it is through the enemy planting negative thoughts in your mind. Planting thoughts like you are fat or too skinny, unattractive, unappreciated, unloved or you will never amount to anything good.

Fear will paralyze you into feelings of despair and rejection and will ultimately lead to isolation. Your perception of yourself is to be alone, saddened until you have become depressed and a social outcast who will no longer function in society.

Fear is the opposite of faith and the beginning of unbelief. You stop believing you exist for a purpose and start to believe your life has no meaning. You no longer have complete confidence, hope or trust in God or anything. Your deliverance from fear and worry is based on you cultivating your faith.

Fear is unbelief, so as unbelief gains strength in your thoughts, fear attacks your emotions. Everyone will have a moment when doubt and worry tries to enter our thoughts. You must understand that you are the controlling element in accepting fear. The enemy is after your future, so fear is your adversary.

God gives us power, love, and a sound mind as the solution to fear. The power of the gospel gives us the strength that comes from knowing we are sons and daughters of God. We can overcome fear and doubt, worry and discouragement through the sustaining power of the love of God, parents, family and friends. The power of a sound mind leads us to see that the gospel is simple, beautiful, logical and transforming.

As we overcome fear, we must walk with confidence and never with arrogance, but with a quiet dignity in our conviction concerning the Savior. When we are confident in our relationship with God we are strong in our emotions, and His perfect love chases out all fear. We will then be able to identify who we are, know our truth and understand our worth.

CHAPTER 5
What I Learned From My Great Grandma

Proverbs 31:31— says, *"Give her of the fruit of her hands; and let her own works praise her in the gates."*

This scripture expresses the praises I have for my Great Grandma, "grandma." She suffered a lot in her lifetime, but she was honest and identified with her struggles in finding her truth and her worth. She was such an overcomer by the word of her testimony and through the power of the precious shed blood of our Savior.

Growing up, I often heard my grandma pray to God for special favors and protection over me. I knew God heard her because I not only believed her words, but I would feel His Presence. My grandma always spoke words filled with life and blessings over my life.

Unfortunately, grandma was never privileged to attend school and could not read nor write; however, she had excellent diction and speech even though she had to rely on her memory and others to read for her. Grandma had a remarkable memory and would recite *Psalms 91* and *Psalms 23* and would often tell me Bible stories. On occasion, I would read the bible to her, but she also encouraged me to read the Bible for myself.

My grandma's love for God and me, helped fuel the passion that later led me to a relationship with Him. She died at the age of *102*, leaving behind a legacy of good words. I enjoyed talking to her and appreciated that she listened and motivated me to be myself and the man I am today.

Here are a few life lessons taught to me by my great grandma:

- She taught me not to be bitter;
- To focus on the good and leave the bad;
- To always rise above a bad or negative situation;
- To always do what is right and seek Him.

I hope you are already privy to these as well and understand them as your truth. Is there someone who leads you closer to the true you?

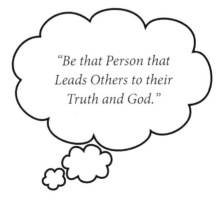

"Be that Person that Leads Others to their Truth and God."

CHAPTER 6
The Reality Is

Whorld were notably the same.
Somethings may have changed during the night, but you and the world still exist. We were given another opportunity to continue to evolve.

It is imperative to understand that you are responsible for defining what you like, and deciding which path you want to travel to reach the outcome you desire. This is an individual and personal process, and only we have control over what fits our pattern.

Even though you are influenced by all kinds of things, you are ultimately still in charge. Reality is defined by Webster's dictionary as *"the quality or state of being real."* First, you have a choice, if you want to live this way or not. Second, you can choose to either make specific plans and work on achieving them or just go with the flow and take life as it is instead of actively trying to shape it; you have a choice.

What I am learning by reflecting on my life is that it is impossible to feel fully satisfied with the extent to which I am making my mark on the earth, particularly when I compare my mark with others. Finding your purpose is an evolutionary process and it can be hard to stay motivated during this process. This means taking steps towards what you want and removing those things in your life that you don't want.

If you are looking for your purpose and passion, stop looking and start doing. Find your joy and appreciate the individual moments to find meaning and significance in everyday life.

The following should be your reality check list:

- Perfect is not real
- Nothing's perfect
- The key to change is accepting who you are and who you are not.
- It is true, everyone has their own struggles.
- Stop judging
- Tell the entire truth
- You already know the truth so stop hiding it.
- Take full responsibility for how you react to others.
- Leave nothing unresolved, surrender and accept what is.
- Become aware of and be sensitive to feelings rather than to ignore them.
- Pay attention to your dreams and visions.
- Forgiveness is a necessary intentional and voluntary decision.

- You choose to love
- Happiness is based on circumstances not necessarily truth.
- Life is what you make it so choose wisely.
- You can be right about the facts and wrong about the truth.
- Ask God for guidance daily, listen and then Obey.
- God is concerned about your life and He wants the best for you.

This is a *"dog-eat-dog"* world driven by survival instincts. We live in a highly competitive ruthless environment without self-restraint, ethics, etc. People will do anything to be successful, even if what they do will harm other people. It is particularly frustrating when others with more power appear to be using their influence to make the world a worst place.

Not everyone is corrupt; you have to listen to your intuition or your ability to understand things immediately without reasoning. You can't live your best life partaking in the mayhem of the world's problems. Each of us have the potential to bring the best of ourselves to a world in need.

CHAPTER 7
Inner Healing

Matthew 11: 28-NIV— *"Come to me, all you who are weary and burdened, and I will give you rest."*

Inner healing is the attempt to free ourselves from the negative emotional effects of harmful experiences. If you understand the cause or root of the problem, then you will accept the remedy. Usually, whatever is going on internally runs deep inside your inner most being to the seat of your soul. I want you to examine your life and get straight to the root of an internal issue to shift your life forever.

Let's look at *John 4:6-19*[2] to review how Jesus handled the woman at the well and shifted her life forever. *[paraphrased]*

A tired Jesus stopped to rest at Jacob's well and while there, saw a woman drawing water and asked her for a drink. Ironically, He had nothing to draw water from the well and even though customarily, Jews did not speak to Samaritans, and it was forbidden for a man to speak to a woman without her husband present; Jesus still engaged her in conversation. I love what He says,

---

[2] *John 4:6-19 KJV and Paraphrased.*

*"to quench her spiritual thirst, the Lord first confessed the truth about water."—**paraphrased**.*

Jesus went on to say, *"Whoever drinks this water will be thirsty again."* Then, He boldly promised, *"Whoever drinks the water I give him will never thirst again."* In one sentence, Jesus shifts from everyday life to everlasting life. Was she ready for that leap of faith; did she want whatever He was offering? *—**paraphrased.***

If we are honest, we get motivated easily to satisfy our physical desires and we overlook our spiritual needs. Jesus asked her to get her husband because it was custom, and she responded, *"I have no husband."* Jesus already knew this, He said, *"Yes and the man you are with is not yours." —**paraphrased.***

His request and answer were more about uncovering truth than about following society's rules. Obviously, her name did not matter because she was merely called the woman at the well. She was more than one of life's outcasts, damaged, and suffering from life's harmful experiences. Instead, what mattered the most to Jesus was that she has a soul; a life of worth and value; that was His main concern. *—**paraphrased.***

Here's the Universal Truth

The woman was probably taking Jesus literally at this point, but He *was not* just talking about regular water. Jesus was comparing the well water to everything that the woman had been thirsting for in life. Her thirst for a man; her thirst for wanting to be loved; and her thirst for simply wanting to be accepted by society.

He was telling her that if she simply drank from Him, then all of those desires for other things that meant her no good, would be washed away. He gave her an invitation to come and drink because He is able to satisfy one's thirst for God and bring inner peace. It's by the workings of the *Holy Spirit* within us that we have an opportunity to progress in our soul toward an even greater wholeness. —*paraphrased*.

Our damaged emotions, will, and thinking, will be transformed by the sanctifying work of the *Holy Spirit* in our lives. As we surrender more and more to the Spirit of God, He will work accordingly in our lives. Like a good father when a child makes a mistake, He is always moved with compassion; and not quickly moved to bring punishment.

We need to get to the root of our problems causing us to feel rejected or to feel unattractive or worthless. At any cost, we must get to the root of our problems or issues. Some people will drink a bottle of whisky or drink a bottle of wine, some will smoke marijuana and some will smoke cigarettes; all looking for answers in the wrong places.

If we would go to the living water (Jesus) and drink, we will no longer thirst or hunger after the things of the world, but instead, after righteousness and holiness. I too looked in the wrong places growing up, I hung out with guys who drank, I partied, went out with ladies, I was searching for answers and trying to fit in somewhere I didn't fit in. You have to look to see why you do the things you do to try and fit in, and why you do the things to try to get rid of a hurt or what was said.

Like the woman at the well, once you get that living water, you don't need the bottle of whisky, you don't need wine, you don't need cigarettes, you don't need to fit in. Instead, you will acutely come to yourself with a new perspective on life and realize that you are wonderfully made, you are created in His Image, and you are His beloved son or His beloved daughter; but keep in mind, it's a process.

The key to begin the healing process and move forward is Forgiveness.

Mark 11:25-26-AMP— "Whenever you stand praying, if you have anything against anyone, forgive him [drop the issue, let it go], so that your Father who is in heaven will also forgive you your transgressions and wrongdoings [against Him and others.] [But if you do not forgive, neither will your Father in heaven forgive your transgressions.]

Having said all that, the real deliverance to healing is linked to us releasing all those little things that once hindered us from going forward, things we didn't like about ourselves, words that were said to us when we were young or even as adults, by our parents, our siblings, family members, and others, you can let it go and forgive them. **You Can Let It Go!**

In spite of the abusive words spoken to me by my mother that were embedded in me and blocked my progress, I had to make a conscious decision in my heart to forgive my mother because she had her own hurt and abuse that she went through not realizing she was hurting her own children and others; remember, hurt people hurt people. More than likely if you came from an environment such as this, your mother and father got hurt from their mother and father and their mother and father got hurt from theirs; a generational curse that can be broken by forgiveness.

To leave you with some good words, you never know what the person right next to you is going through. The scripture says, be kind and affectionate towards one another in so doing you bless that person and you receive a blessing on yourself. Let us speak well of one another and encourage and be uplifting to one another. So be kind and affectionate towards one another.

If you are reading this book and you don't know the Lord, you can to be born again, simply by accepting the Lord and confessing Him as Lord and Savior. Then you can receive forgiveness for your own sins and the ability to forgive those who have hurt you.

One Sunday, Apostle Yvette mentioned that she grew up not knowing her dad and that resonated within me. Maybe, because I still don't have closure on my dad's death. I started asking several family members questions about my dad's death; because inwardly I desired answers to my unanswered questions. This experience allowed me to connect with the importance of releasing our inner pain to God for healing. It also made me able to deal with opening up more regarding my hearing loss.

God created a physical body from the earth and then breathed life into it and the body of man became a living soul. From that point forward, humans have a spiritual nature with a soul within a physical body and whole beings. Each part of us is intricately interwoven with the other parts in a marvelous way. We are a masterpiece just as the body itself is a whole unit made up of many parts, our whole self was created to function as a complete unit. Connect with God, as only He can heal you internally and give you peace.

CHAPTER 8
Comfort Zone Or Movement

Your motto should be, I am always evolving into greatness which is my truth. If your life is not progressively improving then it's time to change what you are doing. Remember, your spirit is always moving you forward so embrace it because your past is just a reminder—your future is bright.

Do you have goals you wish to achieve; are you assessing your life, forming strategies on how to progress? Do you feel at ease where you are in life because it is safe and stress free? Get out of your comfort zone or daze and begin living the life you desire.

Here are some vital daily action steps to ensure power for your movement. Accept who you are at this moment, without doing so, you will constantly feel underserving of your progress. It is normal to struggle and be disappointed in choices you made. It is okay, accept who you are fully, without judgement or blame and move forward.

Remember, you are wonderfully made, right here, right now; Believe it.

- Acknowledge who you are and what you stand for.

- There is no one created like you and it is great being you!
- Define your truth and move on it.
- Figure out what you already know and go beyond fear and denial.
- Let yourself be free to soar and Live it.
- Now that you know your truths, let no one deny it.
- Be honest in your truth.
- Don't hide behind judgement, self, society or anything.
- Your personal truth is just that, truth—so do it loudly and proudly.
- Stay grounded in God's word.

The Word of God is filled with stories of His grace and strength through people of faith. When you choose to study those truths, you will find the nourishment, guidance and hope you need.

Push On

Like a runner, it's difficult to find the motivation to continue when it hurts. It is during these times that you get stronger, it is not easier if you fall. God promises stamina to those who run and those who don't quit when it's hard.

Prayer

Prayer is our direct line to heaven and it is simply talking to God. He wants you to communicate with Him as a person to person phone call. It's easy to talk to someone when you know they love you unconditionally.

Approach Him with confidence and believe that He will deliver you, and you can come boldly to the throne of our gracious God. When you reverence God in faith through worship and when you pray, there is such an expectation that He is going to respond.

Don't wait until you are stuck in a difficult position to be honest in prayer. Prayer is us talking to God and hearing Him pushing us and cheering us on to the finish line.

Trust In God's Plan

We have to know that we are not capable of doing some things on our own, and all things work in His timing and for our good; even if we can't see the end result. God doesn't promise that His plan is easy, but it's beautiful.

Jeremiah 29:11-NIV— *"For I know the plans I have for you, declares the LORD, plans to prosper you and not to harm you, plans to give you a future and a hope."*

God wants to restore us to His original intent and reunite His Spirit with ours and direct us throughout the rest of our lives. Understanding His relentless love will end struggles of self – identity and encourage us to seek Him and search the scriptures, for in them you will find life. You will need to trust the Spirit of God, develop an ear to hear Him through daily prayer.

In closing, feed your mind with good things so you are able to regulate and identify a desirable outcome. Draw from your life experiences whether good or bad and find the true lesson learned. Your truth begins with doing the necessary work; **NO MORE EXCUSES!**

You know what needs to be done, and you already have everything inside of you to identify who you are and to understand your worth and develop your purpose. As you live your truth out loud, those around you will be motivated to do the same.

ACKNOWLEDGEMENT

Thanks to my son Isaiah - a brilliant photographer for the cover photo.

Thanks to my daughter Christine for her encouragement.

Thanks to Kiki Quinton for her pre-editing contribution.

To all those without *apathy* for the hearing impaired or anyone who look different than themselves. Thank YOU because your actions made us strive to improve ourselves and draw from our strengths we did not know already existed inside.

Let's Be Honest With Ourselves is dedicated to everyone who before reading this book struggled with finding their truth, their worth, and understanding their value.

Printed in the United States
By Bookmasters